A BIRCHINGTON VILLAGE ALB

A BIRCHINGTON ROUNDABOUT PUBLICATION

Photographic credits and bibliography
The authors are indebted to the following for the use of photographs from their collections in the production of this book:
   The Birchington Heritage Trust
   Many Birchington Roundabout readers and local residents
   All other photographs are from the Birchington Roundabout collection

The authors would like to thank the following people for their invaluable support and professional contributions
   Jennie Burgess – Parish Archivist
   David Hart – production and design

Bibliography
   The Ville of Birchington by Alfred T Walker published in 1981
   Kelly's Directories 1883-4, 1934, 1938 and 1951

All reasonable steps have been taken to ensure the correct people are credited for the use of their photographs but any issues arising can be addressed to the authors at 25 Alpha Road, Birchington, Kent CT7 9EG who will be happy to make corrections in any future editions.

Introduction

'A Birchington Village Album' forms the third and final publication of our trilogy looking at the wonderful history of Birchington in pictures.

This collection takes the form of a family photograph album with an intriguing assortment of snap shots, which captured the ordinary and extraordinary events that have helped define Birchington's past.

The album includes images of the aftermath of wild storms and extensive coastal erosion, some of the people who joined together in clubs and groups, and the gradual decay and reconstruction of homes and businesses in our village.

The old photographs are set alongside some more recent images to illustrate the changes the village has undergone over the last 100 years - from the subtle evolution of the shops in Station Road, to the dramatic remodelling of our chalk coastline.

The book concludes with a fascinating section featuring advertisements placed in local newspapers and magazines by trades people over the last century - those who offered to provide villagers with a diverse range of products and services, from the purchase of a 'ladies' bicycle', to the enjoyment of 'hygienic milk', and the luxury of an '18-minute laundry service'!

Our coastline has helped define Birchington as a special place to visit, offering a health-giving walk along the beach during winter and a virtually free holiday for locals and visitors alike during the summer, all in a safe environment. These pictures illustrate how throughout the last 100 years many generations have discovered the secret to our success - the beach!

Minnis Bay 1930s. Children from a private school enjoy a short swim

1948. Young ladies demonstrating how to have fun by the sea!

Epple Bay early 1900s

Minnis Bay 1930s

Margery McGinn 1934 Queen of her sand castle

Beresford Gap c.1900

Beach hut owners enjoying Beresford Gap in 1966

Beresford Gap in 2008 from the sea

Beresford Gap c.1900. Wooden beach huts line the slipway

Beresford Hotel above Beresford Gap c.1958

Beresford gap in 2008, popular with water sports enthusiasts

Minnis Bay during the 1950s and (centre) as it looks in 2008 looking westward.

Minnis Bay c.1957

Minnis Bay 1950s

Minnis Bay 2008

Minnis Bay c.1951

Minnis Bay 1950s

Minnis Bay with The Bay Hotel in the back ground during the late 1940s and early 50s. The hotel was demolished during the 1960s then replaced in the late 70s by apartment blocks with much sought after sea views.

Minnis Bay c.1950

Minnis Bay c.1955

Minnis Bay 2008

Minnis Bay 1950

Minnis Bay c.1947

MINNIS BAY, BIRCHINGTON.

Minnis Bay in early 1900s looking east. As the popularity of the car grew so visitors were drawn to Minnis Bay from further afield and finding a parking space became part of a day tripper's routine!

Minnis Bay c.1930

Minnis Bay c.1920

BIRCHINGTON. MINNIS BAY, PROMENADE, LOOKING W.
72294

Minnis Bay c.1920

831 MINNIS BAY, BIRCHINGTON.

Minnis Bay c.1910

Promenade and Beach, Minnis Bay, Birchington
73050

Minnis Bay c.1908

Once the popularity of our beaches had been established the preservation of the cliffs became more important and over the years vast sums of money have been spent holding back nature.

Grenham Bay 1984. Construction starts on new sea defences

Epple Bay 1890s. Construction begins on the slipway, health and safety not yet invented!

Grenham Bay 2008

Minnis Bay 1950s. Repairs required to the sea defences

Grenham Bay 1984 construction works designed to protect the cliffs for future study

Birchington's soft chalk cliffs eroded over the years into fascinating and sometimes strange formations. These cliffs often featured in photos and postcards taken in the 1900s and their notoriety helped popularise the area. Since the construction of the concrete promenade these intriguing sculptures have become a distant memory.

Grenham Bay c.1930

Sebastpool Gap at Grenham Bay 1913

Birchington 1890

Birchington c.1913

King Canute c.1930

Chalk stack c.1910

Chalk stacks between
Grenham and Minnis Bay
1930s

Birchington c.1914

Birchington c.1931

The Cliffs, Birchington-on-Sea 41

The Cliffs Birchington-on-Sea

Epple Bay c.1920s

Coleman Stairs Gap c.1960s

Birchington 1920s

Epple Bay 1912

Keyhole Gap 1930

Cliffs at Grenham 1932

Grenham Bay 1920s

Grenham Bay, now fully protected by extensive concrete promenade, was once a popular beach for families despite the slightly difficult access via wooden steps. One unlucky visitor in 1914 was a whale measuring over 50 feet long, and whose jaw bone was proudly displayed in the garden of The Sea View Hotel.

Grenham Bay 1950s

Grenham Bay 1962

Beached whale at Grenham Bay 1914

Grenham Bay 2008

Grenham Bay 1950s

Grenham Bay 1950s

Minnis Bay has seen its fair share of unusual events over the years from ship wrecks to aeroplane landings! Local man, Ted Brace made an unscheduled visit in April 1969 surviving the experience to the intrigue of local dog walkers. An unwelcome storm in 1978 wreaked havoc with the promenade and private beach huts.

Minnis Bay 1978

Minnis Bay 1969

Minnis Bay 1969

Minnis Bay 1978

Minnis Bay 1978

Colder winters of the 1890s gave Minnis Bay an Arctic look, which didn't bode well for the area's tourist industry! Similar events were repeated in the 1940s and 1960s, despite this Minnis Bay still remains a popular summer attraction.

Birchington 1891

Birchington 1891

Minnis Bay 1891

Minnis Bay 1963

Epple Bay's imposing brick retaining wall is virtually unique in the area, as concrete was quickly adopted to protect our coastline. Above Epple Bay the soil was stripped away by Major Powell-Cotton's labour force to make house bricks, dried on site and probably fired in local kilns.

Epple Bay 2008

Epple Bay 1919

Epple Bay brick fields c.1910

Epple Bay brick fields c.1910

Epple Bay brick fields c.1910

Access to the beaches often began with faults in the cliffs being widened by local people keen to collect the seaweed which regularly washed up on the beaches. The seaweed was sold to local farmers as fertiliser. By the 1870s innovative "bungalows" were being built along the cliff top and a few constructed their own steps down to the beach. Renowned artist Solomon J. Solomon went one step further and had his studio built into the cliff which still stands today, sadly in a bad state of repair.

Coleman stairs Gap c.1900

Coleman stairs Gap 1919

Remains of Solomon J. Solomon's studio 2008

Coleman stairs Gap 2008 from the sea

In the late 1890s the effect of the healthy sea air inspired George Cousins to establish his Seabreeze Cycle business close to the station. His bicycles were the first to be specifically designed for ladies. Mr Cousins' business was evidently successful as he eventually became the proud owner of the first motor car in the village.

An announcement from the early 1900s

BICYCLING FOR LADIES.—In consequence of the Hall-by-the-Sea being required for concerts, &c., Bicycling Lessons will only be given at Birchington-on-Sea, or by arrangement at Westgate-on-Sea.—Seabreeze Cycles, the pioneer of ladies bicycling, manufactory, Birchington, Kent, adjoining the L.C. & D. Railway.

Seabreeze Cycles c.1900

Seabreeze Cycles 1890

SEABREEZE CYCLES

The Popular Exhibit of the Stanley Cycle Shows.

❋

The Novelties for 1894 are the new Patent Spring Frame applied to either Ladies or Diamond Framed Bicycles.

The Ladies' Tandem Bicycle.

The Anti-Hump Diamond, the winner of the Principal Races at the Hall-by-the-Sea.

The Pearl Seabreeze, The Fairy Seabreeze, Ladies' Bicycles.

--❊-- THE SEABREEZE ALUMINIUM ROLLER SKATE WHEELS --❊--
(Undetachable).

The Seabreeze claims to be the pioneer of Ladies' Bicycling, the Seabreeze being the first and only Exhibit at the Stanley Shows to bring before the public the suitability of Bicycling for Ladies. This is no mere brag but is a fact.

GEORGE COUSINS, Patentee & Manufacturer,
BIRCHINGTON-ON-SEA, KENT.

Seabreeze Cycles 1890

The Quex Velocipede pictured in the 1930s

Walker's cycle shop window display in Station Road 1930s

Former location of Seabreeze Cycles now Christies Wine Bar 2008

Commercial vehicles in Birchington.

Jenner's Garage vehicle parked in their yard 1930s

Community Kitchen delivery vans outside their premises - 205 Canterbury Road 1925

Fasham's delivery truck in Station Road 1928

Royal Mail van during the 1920s outside the Post Office in The Square

Private transport.

1951 Martin Pantony aged 4 at Minnis Bay proudly demonstrates his first three-point turn

Central Garage in Station Road in 1982 just before it was demolished and replaced by shop units.

c.1910-20

A family day out from Leslie Road in the 1930s

The Taplin family car in the 1950s in St Mildred's Avenue

In the early 1900s Birchington Motor Engineering Works was established in The Square later trading as Jenners. Over the years it offered services of a fleet of taxis, the sale of new and second hand cars, servicing and repairs. In 2005 The Vehicle Centre was demolished to make way for Alfred Court.

Birchington Engineering works proudly displaying its fleet of taxis in the 1920s

1920s village taxi

Alfred Court constructed in 2005

Canterbury Road looking towards Westgate c.1920

The Vehicle Centre 1999

Public transport in the form of buses and trains has played an important role in the development of Birchington. From the 1900s horse drawn buses carried visitors and locals between towns and The Square became an important terminus.

The Square in 1915 with a motor bus heading towards Westgate and a horse drawn carriage heading into history!

The Square in 1923 with an early open top bus

The family from Quex in The Square in 1908 not requiring public transport

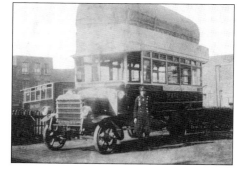

Due to the shortage of petrol during WWII some local buses were converted to run on town gas, which somewhat obscured the view for those travelling on the top deck!

An early car in The Square in 1907

In 1863 Birchington acquired a railway station and the scene was set for Birchington's rapid growth as the trains brought visitors and property developers from London. In 1878 the station acquired its 'on-sea' suffix and Birchington became a recreational destination.

Major Percy and Mrs Hannah Powell Cotton return to Birchington in 1907 after their two year honeymoon in Africa

The Station House in 2008

The Station in the 1950s

The Station in 1910

The Station in 2008

The Station in the 1890s before the footbridge was built

To satisfy the demand of the growing number of visitors to the area several hotels were constructed. Built in 1905 The Bay Hotel occupied perhaps the best location overlooking the bay and enjoying the glorious sun sets which artist J.M.W.Turner found so alluring. By the 1930s Uncle Tom's Cabin had become a popular addition to the facilities available at Minnis Bay with its unique natural timber décor.

The Bay Hotel 1907

The Bay Hotel 1909 looking west

The site in 2008

ADVERTISEMENTS.

WHERE TO STAY AT BIRCHINGTON.

THE BAY HOTEL,

BIRCHINGTON-ON-SEA.

(The only Hotel on Sea-Front.)

This Hotel is of modern construction, and is the most up-to-date Hotel in Birchington.

For Tariff apply to the Resident Manageress.

Telephone No. 42, BIRCHINGTON.

Advert from 1909

7 BIRCHINGTON-ON-SEA. — The Bay Hotel. — LL.

The Bay Hotel in 1910

The Bay Hotel 1931

Uncle Tom's Cabin 1953

Uncle Tom's Cabin 1953

MAKE YOUR WAY TO MINNIS BAY

Get Acquainted with

Uncle Tom's Cabin

Wine   Food   Music

Dance to . . . Sing to . . . Listen to . . .

MOLLY FORBES   **COLIN KEITH**

Top-Ten broadcasting   Brilliant pleasing
organist   pianist

DANCING AND MUSICAL ENTERTAINMENT
EVERY EVENING IN A UNIQUE AND
FRIENDLY ATMOSPHERE : 8 to 10.30 p.m.
Special evenings Wednesday and Saturday, with late bar
extensions

TAKE YOUR CHOICE AT THE BARS: WE ARE A FREE HOUSE
— Large car park. Frequent bus service to our doorway —

It's Unique

UNCLE TOM'S CABIN

Thanet 41235

G68

Advert from 1950s

Uncle Tom's Cabin 1953

Aerial view of The Beresford Hotel c.1930

In 1887 Major W. Morrison Bell purchased two of the first bungalows ever built in this country, joining them together with a large conservatory he created a wonderful family home overlooking the sea. Re-named Beresford Lodge, after its new owner in 1900, and officially listed as a hotel in 1920, having been used as a hospital during World War I. To telephone for a hotel reservation one was to dial 20.

The original two bungalows, Thor and Haun, in 1885

The Beresford Hotel entrance at Beresford Gap c. 1911

THE "BERESFORD HOTEL"
BIRCHINGTON-ON-SEA, KENT

TELEPHONE: THANET 41345   R.A.C. & A.A. ★★★★

The Beresford, reopened in 1950, is again established as One of Britain's Fine Hotels.

Six acres of sea-girt grounds provide you with Hard Tennis Courts, Squash Courts, Putting Course and Private Promenades with direct access to the Bathing Beach. Lock-up Garages.

First-class Golf Courses, Riding Stables and Kennels are all in the vicinity, and picturesque Canterbury only twelve miles distant.

Indoors you will find a magnificent Restaurant and Ballroom facing the Sea. Cocktail Bar. Spacious Lounges and a Recreation Room. A Table for the Epicure and a Cellar for the Connoisseur will leave you with no option to becoming yet another Beresford devotee.

Thor and Haun now joined together in 1887

The Morrison Bell family in 1887

Tennis Court at Thor and Haun c.1890

Organ in the music room c.1890

Billiard Room c.1890

Library c.1890

Troops convalescing at Christmas 1917 before Beresford Hotel formally opened

BERESFORD HOTEL

Advertisement feature for the Beresford Hotel during the 1960s

Beresford Hotel 1922

Beresford Hotel 1930

2006 - The hotel was demolished in 1966 and the site developed into a fifty-unit housing estate in 1971 becoming Moray Avenue and St Magnus Close

Beresford Hotel from sea 1950

Beresford site looking east 2008

For 107 years Birchington could boast that it possessed the only original single storey hotel in the country. Having no stairs was surely a popular feature and it was situated to benefit from the influx of visitors the railway facilitated. The hotel was designed by John Seddon, who had built several bungalows in Birchington which were the first in Britain. It was finally demolished in 1987 to make way for Bierce Court, which offers 40 two bedroom flats with the benefit of optional warden assistance.

In 1909, the innovative Hotel was almost 30 years old

Bungalow Hotel in 1914

Bungalow Hotel. Birchington

Advert from c.1905

Advert from 1958

Residents relaxing outside the Bungalow Hotel 1914

Situated over looking Grenham Bay the Cliff Guest House enjoyed an uninterrupted view of the sea and easy access to the cliffs. Visitors could gain refreshment in the Tudor style tea rooms whilst contemplating an invigorating swim or paddle! The property still stands today as Grenham Bay Court and is a care home for the elderly.

Cliff Guest House c.1930

Cliff Guest House

Cliff Guest House

Tea rooms at the Cliff Guest House

For the more mobile visitor to the area Court Mount Caravan park offered itself as "the finest site on the Kent coast"

Court Mount Caravan park advertisement 1947. Now a static caravan park with many permanent residents

One of the oldest pubs in Birchington originally known as the New Inn. In 1823 it was renamed The Powell Arms in honour of Squire Powell of Quex who was made High Sheriff of Kent in that year.

Side view of The Powell Arms 1960s

The Powell Arms 1950s

The Powell Arms 1950s

The Powell Arms 1947

The Powell Arms 1920s

The Queen's Head can also boast a long history in the village and gave local drinkers the choice of whether to cross The Square or not for over 100 hundred years, before finally being converted to residential use in 2005.

Queens Head Hotel 1909. The Grant memorial drinking fountain opening service is being conducted by the Rev.H.A.Serres.

Advert from 1903

Queens Head Hotel 1905

Queens Head Hotel 1964

A post card from the 1950s

From 1840 this pub was called The New Inn and remained so until the 1960s when it was renamed The Pewter Pot. It then briefly became The Three Legged Toad in 2004 until reverting back to The Pewter Pot. In 2008 the building awaits yet another new name.

The New Inn c.1905

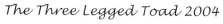
The Three Legged Toad 2004

The Pewter Pot 1970

The New Inn 1920s

The Pewter Pot 1964

Other licensed premises around the village include The Minnis at Minnis Bay where a drinker can enjoy the sunsets, the Acorn Inn in Park Lane and the Sea View Hotel, originally known as the Railway Hotel due to its proximity to the station.

The Acorn Inn advertising wines and spirits of the best quality in 1903

The Minnis 1972

ACORN INN,
Birchington - on - Sea.
◆
CHARLES E. SOLLEY,
Proprietor.
◆
SHEPHERD, NEAME & Co.'s
Faversham
Ales and Stouts on
Draught and in
Bottle.

WINES and SPIRITS . .
of the BEST QUALITY.

1930s advert for The Sea View Hotel

Sea View Hotel,
BIRCHINGTON.
FRANK PROBYN, Proprietor.

Premier Hotel in Birchington.
Billiards. - - Tariff Moderate.
Private Suites of Rooms for Families.
Good Garden and Stabling.

WEEK-ENDS (Saturday Evening to Monday Morning) 15/-

The Minnis 1930's showing the veranda which had seating for patrons

The Sea View Hotel shown in the 1920's but dating back to c.1865

Birchington's renowned variety of commercial ventures dates back well over 150 years with many of these business premises still utilised today by local traders. With the coming of the railway many businesses grew up close to the station to take advantage of passing travellers and Station Road became a focal point of commerce.

Station Road towards Dog Acre c.1960

Alpha Road c.1910 looking from Station Approach

45657. BIRCHINGTON-ON-SEA: ALPHA ROAD.

Looking up Station Road showing Dog Acre on the left c.1900

Station Approach 2008

Station Approach 1964

Built originally as a Temperance Hotel in Victorian times, where alcoholic beverages were banned, the building remained 'tea-total' when it was converted into a dairy for Willett's of Monkton Farm. It was later taken over by Weston's Dairies and is currently trading as a fish and chip shop.

Weston's Dairies 1964

Temperance society certificate 1913

Temperance Hotel 1909

Dairy 1910

Bella Vista Temperance Hotel 1903-04

In 2007 Barclays bank suffered the modern phenomena of a ram raid when thieves attempted to steal the cash machine. The adjoining shops were shaken but not deterred and soon continued trading as they have done for the last 100 years.

A break-in at Barclays Bank 2007

Station Road 2008

United Serviceman's club 1965

Bowketts Cakes proudly positioned in Station Road 1965

1964 on the former site of the entrance to Woodford House School

1930s showing the entrance to Woodford House School which closed in 1961

Entrance to Woodford House School 1930s

Holton & Co 1932 now part of Courts Pharmacy

Station Road 1907

In 1964 R.C.Tibble boldly describes this business as 'The Man's Shop'

Station Road in 2008

For nearly 50 years Barrows offered from the "Corner House" many practical items such as shoes, leather goods, china, glass and sports equipment. But for many Birchington children, Barrows represented wonder and delight as the basement housed a well-stocked toy shop.

Corner House 1953

Barrow's window 1953

Advert from 1930s offering furniture and wirelesses

WE ARE ABLE TO SUPPLY YOUR HOLIDAY NEEDS FROM THE FOLLOWING DEPARTMENTS:

Boot Dept.	Sports Dept.	China & Glass
FASHION SHOES :: SANDALS :: BATHING SHOES LOTUS - DELTA and "K" AGENTS.	TENNIS RACKETS SQUASH RACKETS - CRICKET BATS - GARDEN FURNITURE	A LARGE SELECTION OF STOCK PATTERNS FOR YOUR BUNGALOW

BARROWS
"CORNER HOUSE"
BIRCHINGTON
TEL. 56

Advert from 1930s

Claude Barrows 1960s, who took over the shop from his father Ernest

Established c.1913 The Wayside Café quickly became a popular watering hole for thirsty shoppers and pictures of the mid 1920s show a dramatic remodelling, suggesting business was booming. The café continued into the 1960s when painted wooden parrots greeted customers! The business finally closed its doors in 1962 to make way for a branch of Woolworth's.

Wayside Café 1921

Station Road with Wayside Café on the left 1931

Wayside Café c.1919

Wayside Café c.1919

Corner of Eastfield Road and Station Road in 2008

The buildings constructed alongside the new branch of Woolworths seemed plain in comparison to what they replaced with exception of the false façade to their first floor which gave the impression of a much larger premises.

Woolworths 1964

False façade above Priceless Discount Store 2008

Henrys 1960's

Pair of pet shops in Station Road 2008

B.J.Pearson & Sons Estate Agents in the 1950s

Palmers confectionist and tobacconist 1964

Station Road 2008

Ledgers greengrocers and House of Cards 1970s

2008 Dress Circle occupying the location of Pearsons

At the half way point of Station Road the distinctive canopy at the corner of Westfield Road has featured in numerous postcards and photographs. The rolled corrugated iron has withstood time and weather and offered respite to shoppers for over 100 years.

Station Road 1925

R.G.Scott & Sons Ltd 'The House for bacon' 1964

The canopy in 2008

Station Road winter of 1955-56

Station Road summer 1906

Birchington's own cinema the Public Hall, but nicknamed 'The Bug Hutch,' showed its first film in 1918 and continued entertaining the villagers and visitors alike until 1961. During these years it was named The Princess, The Select, The Regent, The Ritz and finally The Regal. The building has stood the test of time and was, until recently, a place of worship.

Public Hall Station Road 1950s

Station Road 2008

One of the first adverts for The Public Hall - opened by Mrs Susan Gray in 1902

Peter Read school outfitters 1964 now The Bottle Shop

Thanet House, one of the oldest properties in Station Road and still the home to local thriving businesses.

Thanet House c.1900 draper and supplier of clothes

Thanet House 1964

Thanet House 2008 offering picture frames and hair do's!

Nicholls 1920s selling books and gifts

Station Road 1964

Laburnham House, a grade II listed building built around 1765 with its notable 'Dutch gable' and most likely named after the long lived laburnham tree which overhung Station Road for many years.

Laburnum House 2008

Laburnum House 1960s

Rogers & Co Fishmonger and Poulterer 1920

Fishmongers, Station Road 1930s

Station Road 2008

Hutchinson Jewellers, Station Road 1964

Newsagents in Station Road 1950s demolished in 1970

The bakers adjoining the newsagents in the1930s

An early advert for Charles Maxted family butcher which adjoined Hutchinson Jewellers

The location in 2008

Gardners the greengrocers and seed merchant, corner of
Albion Road 1930s

Rush's Café in The Square 1950

Hayward's shoe shop 1964

Site of Hayward's shoe shop in 2008

The Square 1890 opposite All Saints'
Church on north side of The Square

Brooks Tea Rooms in the early 1920s shared the building with Lloyds bank but by the end of the decade it would appear Lloyds had taken over the whole premises, its occupation continues to this day.

Brooks Tea Rooms in the mid 1920s

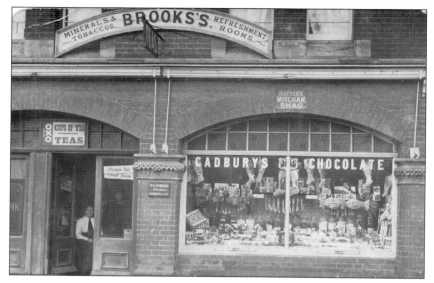

Brooks Tea Room early 1920s

Lloyds Bank late 1920s

Lloyds Bank and The Square in 2008

Approaching The Square from Westgate c.1910

Canterbury Road 1978, a shop occupied this site from 1896 until the late 1970s when it was converted to residential use.

Canterbury Road c.1915

Canterbury Road c.1950

The Square in 2008

c.1915

c.1913

THE POWELL ARMS

QUEEN'S HEAD HOTEL

THE SQUARE BIRCHINGTON ON SEA

c.1950

c.1920

Park Lane c.1910 looking towards The Square

Fountain Cottage, Park Lane 2008

D. GOLDER & SONS, Park Lane, BIRCHINGTON,

General and Furnishing Ironmongers.

Japanners, Hardware, Petroleum Oil Merchants and Petrol Storers.
Patent Safety Lamps, and Repairs ; Incandescent Mantles, Fittings, etc.
Wall Papers, Paints, Stains, Brushes, Lixos, and General Repairs.

Advert for D.Golder & Sons, ironmonger c.1903, in front of Fountain Cottage

Garage in Park Lane during 1930s

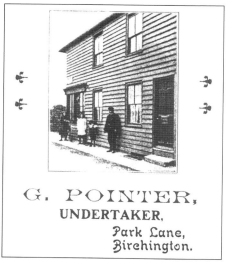

G. POINTER,

UNDERTAKER,

Park Lane,
Birchington.

Advert for G.Pointer,
Undertaker in Park Lane
c.1903

Advert for W.T.Harris, occupying
The Barn, Albion Road c.1903

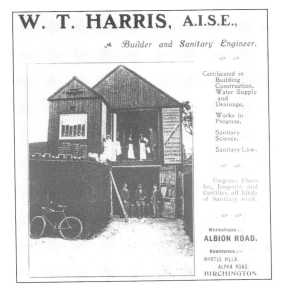

In 2008 the property is yet again
occupied by a plumbers' merchant

Birchington Engineering and the Methodist
Chapel c.1960, demolished in 1988

An aerial view of the cleared
site in 1992

Taplin Court on the former site of Birchington Engineering works in 2008

One of the earliest recorded grocery stores in the village was originally established in 1817 and occupied the building next door to the Queen's Head. In 1964 Vye & Son relocated to the modern premises at the bottom of Station Road. Bought out by the Lipton's chain soon afterwards.

Vye & Son, The Square c.1915

Vye & Son in its second location in Station Road 1964

The former site of Vye & Sons in 2008

Vye & Son, The Square c.1920

Vye & Son adverts from 1920s

The Square in 1964 shown in panorama featuring the Coffee Lounge, a focus for young and old during the 1960s where for sixpence one could listen to the popular songs of the day on the only jukebox in the village.

The Square in 2008

Shops away from Station Road

The Birchington Bay Stores 1903 in Minnis Road

The Gunnersbury General Stores, 317 Canterbury Road 1925

The Gunnersbury Stores 1920

Corner of Alpha Road and Epple Road in 2008

Alpha Stores 1927

Mr Johnson's Old Bay Stores and Post Office, Minnis Road 1940s

Birchington's enviable location beside the sea encouraged the establishment of many private schools where pupils could benefit from healthy sea air which would surely facilitate learning. Queen Bertha's School was established in 1929 by Miss C M Hunt and Miss E Randall-Harris for 'genteel young ladies'. The girls wore distinctive gold and scarlet uniforms. The school was demolished in 1959 and the site developed into a residential estate of bungalows opposite the modern King Ethelbert School.

Queen Bertha's School 1929

Miss C M Hunt and Miss E Randall-Harris early 1950s

Riding Lesson 1940s

Some of the 'genteel girls' of Queen Bertha's in the early 1940s

One of the many schools in Birchington was Woodford House situated about half way down Station Road. The school was built in c.1865 and was originally known as 'The Lawn'. H A Erlebach who founded the school with his brother, Alfred, tragically lost three sons in WWI and donated the recreation ground in Park Road in their memory.

Woodford House School c.1913

Advert for Woodford House School from the 1930s

Woodford House prefects and Mr Albert Hodges, Principal in 1948

Woodford House School c.1920

Woodford House School sack race 1958

Woodford House football team 1948

Woodford House School,
BIRCHINGTON.

PRINCIPALS: H. A. ERLEBACH, B.A., F.L.S., F.R.G.S.
ALBERT HODGES, L.C.P.
Thorough Education in most healthy surroundings.

Advert from c.1920

The school was demolished in 1961 and the site redeveloped into Woodford Court shown here in 2006

Grenham House school was constructed in 1910 although originally founded in 1901 in Minnis Road by Henry Jeston and Bernard Ransome. The Grenham Road school boasted swimming pool, tennis court and spacious playing fields. When the school was finally demolished in 1985 the playing fields became the Hunting Gate estate.

Grenham House 1910

Grenham House tennis court c.1965

Grenham House 1971

Grenham House c.1925

Grenham House cricket pavilion c.1950

For the less privileged children Park Lane School has provided an excellent education for over 150 years. (Laming Road was named after Headmaster Mr Charles Laming who was principal in the 1930s). The school continues to thrive as Birchington Church of England Primary School with over 400 children.

Park Lane School 1929

Park Lane School 1950s

Park Lane School 1950s

Park Lane School 1920

Park Lane School 1929

Frozen sea at Minnis Bay with Reculver towers in the distance, winter 1891-92

Damage to Minnis Bay in 1897 after severe storm

BIRCHINGTON BAY FLOODED.—DESTRUCTIVE EFFECTS OF THE STORM. From a Sketch by Miss FELICIA WAIN.

Snow storm in 1891 blocks Minnis Road (looking towards village)

The Dip at Minnis Bay flooded in the storms of 1953

Train snow bound just outside Birchington in winter 1891-92

Epple Bay, early 1963 when the ice extended along the North Kent coast for seven miles (see also page 15)

Flooded Station Road 1930

King Edward Road 1959

Cross Road, winter 1955-56

Flooded house in Canute Road 1953

Birchington has held a carnival each year since 1932 with the exception of the war years. Residents entered into the spirit of the event with great enthusiasm, with marching bands, beauty queens and local businesses publicising themselves with highly decorated floats. Money collected along the route was donated to charity.

Float advertising another popular local event, Quexpo, in 1976

Comical fireman 1956 taken in Albion Road

Birchington Guild of Players float with 1920s theme - mid 1980s

Carnival performer outside International Stores in The Square 1960s

St Johns Ambulance joining in the fun 1956

Carnival prize winner Owen Hart in 1938

Parade of beauties in Albion Road 1956

Miss Birchington and Princesses in 1982

Miss Birchington and her court 1956

The Birchington Guild of Players

Rev Grenville Sharpe founding member of the Birchington Guild of Players pictured here in 1939

Production in late 1930's

The Boyfriend 1982 produced at the Village Centre where the Guild currently perform most of their productions

An open-air production of 'A Mid Summer Night's Dream' at Quex Park in 1978

The old Church House on the corner of Kent Gardens and Canterbury Road was the venue for Guild productions until it was demolished in 1972

Woodchurch Farm workers in the 1950s

Gentlemen revellers in 1938 call at Birchington, pictured outside the Powell Arms

Woodchurch Farm workers and families having a day out in the 1950s

Woodchurch Farm workers enjoying a little too much Cobb & Co's Margate beer in the 1930s

Dante Gabriel Rossetti was one of the founders of the Pre-Raphaelite Brotherhood. He came to Birchington on 5th February 1882; already a sick man he sadly died two months later on 9th April. He spent the last few weeks of his life in a property later known as Rossetti Bungalow, located between Beach Avenue and Rossetti Road, loaned to him by his friend John P Seddon, architect of our famous Bungalow Hotel.

Rossetti window in All Saints Church, the left light being a reproduction of his painting of the Passover

Rossetti Bungalow pictured in the late 1920s

Rossetti's head stone in All Saints Churchyard

Dante Gabriel Rossetti pictured in 1862

Rossetti and his family in 1862

In the past Birchington fielded not only a men's cricket team but also a ladies' team and judging by this photograph were compelled to wear a skirt which must have made bowling and running difficult!

Birchington Ladies Cricket team 1920s

Birchington Cricket team 1936

Birchington Cricket team 1950s

Birchington Cricket team 1909

5th Birchington Brownie Pack with their Brownie
Queen in 1974

Birchington Brownie May Queen 1965 in front of the Powell Arms

Brown Owl looks on as the May Queen approaches the
church in 1965

Maypole and onlookers await dancers in The Square 1965

Scouts get lucky as they pull a
May Queen 1965

Birchington Scouts at camp in 1926

Scouts on parade in The Square c.1920

Birchington Scouts proudly pose in 1926

A 1932 group of Birchington Scouts

For over 100 years Minnis Bay has been the focus for the Children's Special Service Mission (CSSM) now known as Scripture Union. Each summer for two weeks in August young people join together to worship and socialise in a safe and friendly environment.

Minnis Bay CSSM late 1930's

Children Special Service Mission 1900 Minnis Bay

A 'sand altar' marks the focus point of CSSM in 1965

The congregation fills the beach and promenade for a popular service in 1913

St Thomas' Church, Minnis Road built in 1932, the choir pictured here in 1964

Birchington Methodist Church, built in 1830, located close to The Square and seen here in the 1920s

A joyful Confirmation group, All Saints' Church, 1960

Birchington choir boys 'Beating the Bounds' in 1935

The Reverend Grenville Sharp and choir of All Saints' Church 1939

Barnes Wallis tested his ingenious bouncing bombs between Minnis Bay and Reculver during WWII and in 1973 several were recovered from sea bed

Troops in Station Road in 1943. That year troops were billeted in The Bay, Bungalow and Beresford Hotels

Local Land Army girls Peggy and Amy May working at Brooksend Farm in 1942

Naval Officer, Lord Charles Beresford pictured in 1910 was proprietor of the Beresford Hotel

Soldiers billeted at 24 Alfred Road during World War II

Birchington on Sea Fire Brigade in 1913

Village Police Constable Herbie Flower pictured in 1971

Post office workers in 1959 at the Albion Road sorting office

In 1902 Firemen and Lifeboat men were trained to carry out both duties. Pictured outside 'The Anchorage,' now Geoffrey Court, in Alpha Road

Coast Guards Firing party on parade at Birchington Station 1913

George Willshire
at The Dip c.1946

The first Vicar of Birchington Rev
Alcock, on the right, outside All Saints
Church c.1880

c.1880 In The Square looking towards Mill Lane with
the windmill in the distance

1933 Mrs Sayer outside the Alms Houses, now
Anvil Close area not far from The Square

Local business woman, Mrs Hudson, with her three daughters c.1920

Local girls collecting sweet peas in Acol in 1906

Two local lovelies apparently for sale! Grenham Gap c.1926

'Nan' Owen at Minnis Bay in the 1920s taking the air

Quex Park Estate

Home to the Powell-Cotton Family Quex mansion was built in 1808 although a house has stood on the site since the early 1400s. A museum adjoins the house which displays a private collection of African wildlife, skilfully preserved, that has become world renowned as a unique source of original DNA. The estate has been an invaluable employer for local people for generations and still holds many major events in the grounds.

The tree lined avenue approaching the mansion during the 1930s

7. The Mansion, Quex Park, Birchington.

The Powell-Cotton family carriage c.1900

The Waterloo Tower constructed in 1818 which houses 12 bells

The Powell-Cotton family were keen photographers and much of the estate and its day to day workings were recorded, including these farmhands in 1913

Bellringers at Quex probably called upon to ring the only 12 peal of bells in Kent other than Canterbury Cathedral c.1900

The Sea Tower or Observatory constructed in 1814 as a lookout and signalling station

Advert for Big Game and Curios at the museum in 1929

Fete held in the grounds July 1929

"A Triumph in Artistic Arrangement"

EXHIBITION
OF
BIG GAME AND CURIOS
(LECTURES BY THE CURATOR).

The Largest Known Collection Shot by One Man.
Whole Animals Grouped in their Natural Surroundings.

OPEN TO VISITORS—
July, August and September : Wednesdays and Thursdays, 2.30—6.
Other Months : Thursdays, 2.30—4.30

THE POWELL-COTTON MUSEUM
QUEX PARK - BIRCHINGTON

ADMISSION (No Tax) 1/-   Children (under 12) 6d.
Only Entrance by Quex Farm Gate, Park Lane, Birchington.
MOTOR 'BUSES.—Margate Harbour to Birchington, every 10 minutes.

1929 - 30

Quex gardeners c.1890

Summer Fete in 1929 held in the grounds at the rear of the mansion

Charles Spurgeon, a charismatic Baptist preacher, created an orphanage in Stockwell in 1869. Many of the children suffered ill health so it was decided to open a branch by the sea. In 1917 Birchington Hall Estate with its 40 acres was purchased and by the 1960s Spurgeons Homes housed over 200 children.

Resident boys with their 'house parents' in 1960

Aerial view of Spurgeons adjoining Canterbury Road and Park Road, now the site of Birch Hill Park housing development

The Nursery building c.1960, converted to flats during the redevelopment in the 1980s

Revered Charles Haddon Spurgeon who died in 1892

Birchington Hall c.1920

Birchington Hall c.1930

St Mary's Convalescent Home opened in Beach Avenue in 1888. Unique in care homes, St Mary's had its own chapel. For most of its working life the home offered recuperation from illness but after the site was redeveloped in 2006/07 it now offers luxury retirement apartments.

St Mary's Convalescent Home c.1930 from Beach Avenue

The home c.1930 seen from Rossetti Road

Nurses from St Mary's c.1925

Dining Room c.1930

Cleared site of St Mary's in 2007

2008 St Mary's Lodge warden assisted retirement apartments

Located in Cross Road, The Thicket, built in 1900, owned by Dr Cross was run as a convalescent home providing much needed beds for the wounded fighting the Boer War. In the 1914-18 war the house became a full time hospital. The property was demolished in 1967.

The Thicket c.1900

Rear view 1930s

The Thicket in 1905 showing the level crossing, now replaced by a footbridge between Alpha Road and Cross Road

Georgian style houses were built on the site in Cross Road in 1970

Ethelbert Road, Minnis Bay c.1920

Queens Avenue, Minnis Bay 1920

Epple Bay Road 1925

East End Villas, Canterbury Road c.1940

Prospect Road in 1912

Neame Barns c.1880 now replaced by a parade of shops in Canterbury Road

Neame Barns c.1880 located approximately opposite the Methodist Church

Old Bay Cottage, Minnis Road 1937 still standing today

Old Bay Cottage, Minnis Road 1900s with parts dating back to the 15th century

Darby's, corner of Park Lane 1910

Tree lined Beach Avenue looking towards the station c.1930

◄ Empty Coast Guard Cottages c.1945 which once overlooked Epple Bay

Tower bungalows designed and built by John Seddon c.1882

▼ Morrison Bell House, Albion Road built in 1900 as a convalescent home for delicate children. Replaced in the 1960s with Georgian style semi-detached houses

◄ The Coach House, Spencer Road in 2006, built c.1882. Sgraffito work by George Frampton who designed the Peter Pan statue in Kensington Gardens, London

◄ Wild Air in Cliff Road overlooking Beresford Gap, built in the 1920s, replaced by a luxury apartment block in 1998

Carmel Court built in 1895 in Spencer Road said to have been a replica of a villa near Mount Carmel in Palestine. Demolished in 1964 and replaced by a block of flats

Court Mount, Canterbury Road seen here in 1963 has parts of the building dating back to 16th Century. Now converted into flats

Orion, Nasmith Road in 1960

Minnis Road looking towards the sea in 1926

Coast Guard Station in 1913 with coastguard cottages behind which can still be found in Grenham Bay Avenue

Advertising one's business in a local newsletter, newspaper or magazine has been an imperative since the invention of printing. This collection of advertisements offers a unique insight to the social history of their time.

The very earliest advertisers seem less inhibited by political correctness and were happy to offer themselves as the largest or the best of their kind, and the claims for the benefits of their products were often bold and unequivocal.

In the sixties and seventies adverts were more constrained due to the growing cost of space within publications and ever increasing number of rules which prevented outrageous claims - such as the health-giving properties of smoking!

Whilst many of the featured businesses and products may have vanished from our village, they have left intriguing footnotes to their stories, which offer us a traceable address and a pithy description of themselves.

These often tiny adverts neatly recorded their contribution to village life, supplying us with a potted history of how they traded, where they traded and to whom they traded. Overall a wonderful typographical snapshot of our village history!

Smokers' 'Fur'

How to detect it—How to prevent it

Try this now. Run your tongue round your mouth—do you notice it ... a rough woolly feeling? Smokers' fur has got a hold, and is staining your teeth.

Protect Teeth with toothpaste containing
★ 'MILK OF MAGNESIA'

Dentists know smokers' fur is caused by excess acid in the mouth. Kill the acid and you shift the fur. 12,000 dentists say ' Milk of Magnesia ' is the most effective antacid known. They recommend smokers to use the toothpaste containing ' Milk of Magnesia ' — t h e o n l y toothpaste containing it—Phillips' Dental Magnesia. Get a tube of Phillips' Dental Magnesia and clean your teeth with it each night and morning. Then you'll feel the difference : you'll have teeth which look clean, feel clean, are clean ; a sweet mouth to give new zest to smoking.

1/1d. and 1/10½d.   Sold everywhere.

RETURN EMPTY TUBES TO THE CHEMIST.

WAR SAVINGS CAMPAIGN

For her bottom drawer?

Vera : She's always swanking about her boy friend in the R.A.F. — I sometimes wonder what *he* thinks, though.

Jane : What about ?

Vera : Well — she spends too much on herself. If you had a friend in the Forces would you think that playing the game ?

Jane : I don't know. Why not ?

Vera : Well — for one thing we want more planes. The least she should do is to put everything she can into War Savings and help pay for them. After all, she can get it back with interest — and it will come in jolly handy when they get married.

Don't Spend—DO Lend

Go to a Post Office or your Bank or Stockbroker and put your money into 3% Savings Bonds 1955-1965, 2½% National War Bonds 1946-1948, or 3% Defence Bonds; or buy Savings Certificates; or deposit your savings in the Post Office or Trustee Savings Banks. Join a Savings Group and make others join with you.

For Prompt Repairs and All Accessories

BIRCHINGTON CYCLE STORES

Proprietor : A. J. SHARP.

Agent for "HERCULES" Cycles

Special attention given to Tradesmen's Cycles.

Hitler will send no warning — *so always carry your gas mask*

ISSUED BY THE MINISTRY OF HOME SECURITY

The Snowdrift Hand Laundry

PADDOCK ROAD
OFF STATION ROAD.

The LAUNDRY for HIGH-CLASS WORK

NO CHEMICALS USED.

A Noteworthy Local Industrial . . Establishment . .

Proprietress :—
Mrs. A. M. GAMBRILL.

. . . *"the very centre of sunshine"*

ROSSVILLE COURT
SPENCER ROAD, BIRCHINGTON-ON-SEA, KENT.
A Guest House of Distinction.
" *On the grass of the cliff*
By the edge of the steep "
A well-appointed and tastefully decorated house-by-the-sea, bathed in sunshine.

Spacious lounge and dining room facing the sea. H. & C. running water, gas fires and well-sprung beds in all bedrooms ; a bathroom adjoins each. The secluded walled garden—where tea may be enjoyed on the very edge of the cliff—overlooks the beach with extensive sea views ; bathing from the house. Tonic air ; high sunshine record ; low rainfall.

The ideal surroundings for a REAL rest cure

TELEVISION   OPEN ALL THE YEAR   PUTTING GREEN
(Special Winter Terms)

Resident Proprietress   Telephone
Mrs. R. E. BLAKEMORE   Birchington 468

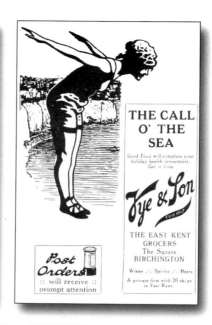